gift of Bob + Penny Boysen, Christmas 1999

Everything
Starts
from
Prayer

Everything Starts from Prayer

MOTHER TERESA'S MEDITATIONS ON SPIRITUAL LIFE FOR PEOPLE OF ALL FAITHS

SELECTED AND ARRANGED BY ANTHONY STERN, M.D.

WITH A FOREWORD BY LARRY DOSSEY, M.D.

WHITE CLOUD PRESS
ASHLAND, OREGON

10 9 8 7 6 5 4 3 2 1

First edition: October 1998
Printed in the United States of America
This edition is printed on acid-free paper

Cover design: Daniel Cook Design, Santa Cruz, California
Cover photo: Magnum Photos, Inc. © 1997 Raghu Rai

Photo credits: All photos courtesy of Magnum Photos, Inc.
Photographs on pages xx, 16, 32, 66, and 104 by Raghu Rai.
Photograph on p. 96 by Martine Franck

LIBRARY OF CONGRESS CATALOGING-IN-PUBLICATION DATA
Teresa, Mother, 1910-1997
    Everything starts from prayer : Mother Teresa's meditations on
spiritual life for people of all faiths / selected and arranged by
Anthony Stern : with a foreword by Larry Dossey.
        p.   cm.
    Includes bibliographical references.
    ISBN 1-883991-25-0
    1. Meditations. I. Stern, Anthony. II. Title
    BX2182.2.T384   1998
    248.3'2-DC21   98-11855
                                                CIP

TABLE OF CONTENTS

Foreword

Larry Dossey, M.D.

P RAYER IS ONE OF THE ESSENTIAL activities of human life. Throughout history it has nurtured our grandest visions and provided meaning and purpose to our activities. It is impossible to imagine the evolution of any culture without prayer. Prayer is universal; we know of no society in which it does not take place.

Prayer has many faces. There are prayers of petition, intercession, thanksgiving, and adoration. But one thread connects all prayer: Whatever form it may take, *prayer is a bridge to the Absolute,* a way of connecting with something higher, wiser, and more powerful than the individual self.

Many people believe that prayer is old-fashioned in our modern, scientific age, that prayer and science are incompatible, and that prayer belongs to the category of superstition and fantasy. One of the great ironies of the modern age, however, is that proponents of prayer and proponents of science are engaged in a new and amazing dialogue. This is happening in three different ways.

First, a high proportion of scientists today believe in a Supreme Being who answers prayer. This may come as a shock to people who have been taught that genuine scientists cannot simultaneously believe in the Absolute and do good science. In 1997, however, researchers surveyed American biologists, physicists, and mathematicians about their religious beliefs.[1] They found that 39% believe in God—specifically, they believe in the kind of God who responds to prayer. The highest percentage of believers was found among mathematicians, who practice what many consider the purest kind of science that exists. And so we see that the prevalent views that science is godless, that atheists make the best scientists, and that prayer and science cannot coexist are simply stereotypes to be challenged.

Second, medical scientists studying the effects of prayer have found compelling evidence of the benefits of prayer, meditation, and relaxation on individuals who pray.[2] The body appears to *like* prayer and responds in healthy ways in the cardiovascular, immune, and other systems. But even more interesting are studies showing that intercessory or *distant* prayer also has an effect, even when the individual being prayed for is unaware of the prayer being offered and is at a great distance from the person prayering. These studies are numerous, have been replicated by many scientists, and have involved not only humans but nonhumans as the prayer recipients. This latter point is important: If prayer's effects extend to animals and plants, they cannot be ascribed only to positive thinking or the placebo response.

The third major development heralding a synthesis of science and prayer is the recent emergence of scientific theories on the nature of consciousness.[3] In general, these views go beyond the old idea that the effects of the mind are confined to one's individual brain and body. These new theories permit consciousness to act outside the physical body, perhaps through intercessory prayer. In light of these new ways of thinking about consciousness, it no longer seems outrageous to suggest that prayer might act at a distance to bring about actual changes in the world.

In studies of intercessory prayer, researchers have found no correlation between the religious affiliation of the praying individual and the effects of the prayer. This affirms the view that prayer is universal, that it belongs not just to a specific religion but to the entire human race. These findings sanction the importance of religious tolerance, asking us to honor the prayers and spiritual visions of other religious traditions, no matter how radically they differ from our own.

Although personal religion does not correlate with prayer's effects in experimental studies, there is a quality that does make a great difference. It is a factor that sounds quite old-fashioned: *love*. Without love, the prayer experiments don't work as well, in fact, they often fall flat. As a physician, this finding intrigues me, because healers throughout history have uniformly proclaimed the importance of compassion, caring, and empathy for the patient. The best physicians I know honor the power of love and care in healing. They believe that, while penicillin is powerful, penicillin plus love is more powerful still.

It is on these two issues in particular—the role of religious tolerance and the place of love and compassion in prayer—that I feel especially connected with Mother Teresa's work and writings. As Tony Stern points out in his introduction to this volume, Mother Teresa stated, "I've always said we should help a Hindu become a better Hindu, a Muslim become a better Muslim, a Catholic become a better Catholic."

There is a related story about Mother Teresa that attests to her tolerance, one that I have always adored, although it may be apocryphal. A brash young reporter once asked her, "Are you a saint?" Without hesitating, she poked the young man in the chest with a gnarled finger and said, "Yes, and so are you!"

Mother Teresa would undoubtedly insist that prayer does not need science to validate it, and I would agree. People test prayer every day in their lives, and life is the most important experimental laboratory of all. But, since science is one of the most powerful factors guiding modern life, we would be foolish to disregard what science has to say about prayer, particularly since so many of its comments are positive.

One of the most remarkable trends in modern medicine is the return to prayer.[4] Three years ago, only three medical schools in the United States had courses exploring the role of religion and spiritual practice in health; currently nearly thirty do.[5] First-rate researchers are examining the effects of prayer in healing at various medical schools, hospitals, and research institutions; national conferences linking spirituality and healthcare are becoming routine.

Somewhere, Mother Teresa must be smiling.

Footnotes

1. E. J. Larson, "Scientist are still keeping the faith," *Nature* (April 3, 1997): 345.

2. Larry Dossey, *Healing Words: The Power of Prayer and the Practice of Medicine* (San Francisco: HarperSanFrancisco, 1993).

3. Larry Dossey, "Emerging Theories" in *Be Careful What You Pray For* (San Francisco: HarperSanFrancisco, 1997): 190-92.

4. Larry Dossey, "The return of prayer," *Alternative Therapies* 3:6 (1997): 10ff.

5. Jeffrey S. Levin, David B. Larson, Christina M. Puchalski, "Religion and spirituality in medicine: research and education," *Journal of the American Medical Association* 278 (1997): 792-93.

Larry Dossey, M.D. is Executive Editor of *Alternative Therapies* and author of *Healing Words, Prayer Is Good Medicine,* and *Be Careful What You Pray For.*

Introduction

Anthony Stern, M.D

T HE WOMAN WE ALL KNEW as Mother Teresa was devoutly Catholic and profoundly devoted to Jesus. She expressed her ceaseless devotion in so many ways, central among them her well-known work with the poor and the sick. Less known expressions included her deep respect for all religions and her burning wish for all people to come closer to God. It was with a longing to reach as many souls as possible that she wrote, "I've always said we should help a Hindu become a better Hindu, a Muslim become a better Muslim, a Catholic become a better Catholic." And it was with a practical recognition of what works that she declared, "Everything starts from prayer."

It is in this spirit that the following collection of Mother Teresa's sayings is offered. I've selected and arranged them from many of Mother Teresa's prior writings to give the widest possible access to people with no clear path as well as to those with various inner paths. I have tried to glean pearls of inspiration that provide an ecumenical entry into a life of prayer. And I've framed a host of Mother Teresa's reflections within this topic of prayer.

While Mother Teresa did not fully undertake an entirely universal approach herself, the basic direction she took was shown on the occasion she asked a wealthy person to build a mosque in Yemen, with the plea that the Muslim brothers and sisters there needed a place to meet God.

It is the same direction she took with one of her friends and biographers, Navin Chawla. She knew he was a non-observant, nearly atheistic Hindu, yet not once over the years did she question his beliefs or his religion. But she did repeatedly, some might say incessantly, nudge him with the same question, "Have you begun to pray yet?"

Consider also one of the projects dearest to Mother Teresa's heart: her Homes for the Dying, where every person receives the last rites of his or her own tradition. She was overheard to whisper to one of the terminally ill, "You say a prayer in your religion, and I will say a prayer as I know it. Together we will say this prayer and it will be something beautiful for God." By the early 1980s, 17,000 people had died in these Homes. Seeing the peace and beauty of their deaths, she was sure that all these souls, whatever their faiths or sects, had gone straight to heaven.

For Mother Teresa, prayer was the universal way to God.

Her own spiritual advisor and biographer Edward Le Joly drove this point home, observing that when a journalist approached her at an airport with the request, "Have you a message for the American people?" Mother Teresa didn't say "give more," or even "love one another more." Rather, she answered without hesitation, "Yes, they should pray more."

And so, let's be clear: The book you hold now gives the same answer by the same great spiritual leader and teacher, only in an extended form. Instead of her succinct response amidst the bustle of an airport, you have a set of meditations to be savored slowly in your home. It's a fuller, more developed version of the same basic counsel, the same basic plea: "Pray more."

Everything Starts from Prayer relates more directly to personal and private prayer than to ritual and community prayer. This is fitting, because everything depends on your own beginning. Praying as an individual is no substitute for the spiritual nurturance, sharing, and guidance of communal spiritual practice and service. Yet we need to begin, again and again, on our own, digging within our own ground, making room for the grace that is always available to us. Our rote prayers and our prayers together can have great meaning as a pooling of devotional energies only when they're infused with the fire of individual souls—the sweet and profound energy our own souls release when they've caught fire.

When Dorothy Hunt was considering an idea that ultimately became the lovely Mother Teresa collection *Love: A Fruit Always in Season*, she asked permission to undertake the task. Mother Teresa's reply: "Make it a prayer." Make the very work a prayer. My one suggestion for reading this book is an echo of her's: Make it a prayer. The more seriously and openly you approach it, the more the words will penetrate. The more you bring your whole self to it with unhurried simplicity and receptivity, the more the thoughts and feelings behind the words will touch something deep inside you. And the more fully you connect with your own wish to be in the presence of the Eternal as you read, the more likely it will be that the holy meaning behind the words will spark something real in you.

In her wonderful book *A Simple Path*, Mother Teresa introduced readings from her Order's prayer book by suggesting that readers could replace "Jesus" with "God" in their prayers if they were not Christians. Similarly here, feel free to replace the word "God" with whatever works best for you in referring to a higher power in your life. The same should be urged for Mother Teresa's reference to God as "he" or "him," and of other traditional gender vocabulary herein. Please substitute words you find acceptable if these are off-putting in any way.

Mother Teresa spoke often of how utterly she relied on the power of prayer to connect her to God. Twenty-four hours a day, she'd say. And for emphasis, she sometimes added that if the day were longer, that's how much longer she'd need God's strength through prayer.

But then, what spiritual seeker has not depended on prayer? And what heart has not cried out, and not been better for having done so?

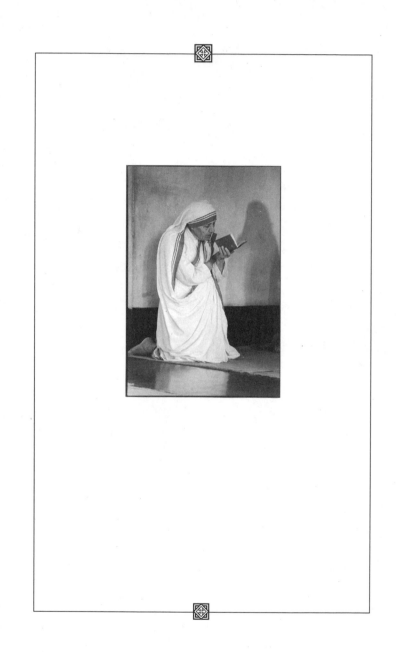

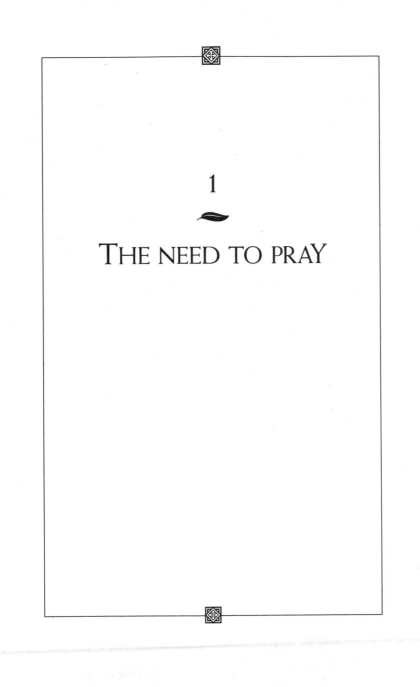

1

THE NEED TO PRAY

E VERYTHING STARTS FROM PRAYER.
Without asking God for love, we
cannot possess love and still less are we
able to give it to others. Just as people
today are speaking so much about the
poor but they do not know the poor, we
too cannot talk so much about prayer
and yet not know how to pray.

The Need
to Pray
~
1
~

YOU MAY BE EXHAUSTED WITH WORK, you may even kill yourself, but unless your work is interwoven with love, it is useless. To work without love is slavery.

❧

PEOPLE THROUGHOUT THE WORLD MAY look different or have a different religion, education, or position, but they are all the same. They are the people to be loved. They are all hungry for love.

I N MOST MODERN ROOMS YOU SEE AN
electrical light that can be turned on by
a switch. But, if there is no connection with
the main power house, then there can be no
light. Faith and prayer is the connection with
God, and when that is there, there is service.

W E HAVE TO POSSESS BEFORE WE CAN give. He who has the mission of giving to others must grow first in the knowledge of God. He must be full of that knowledge.

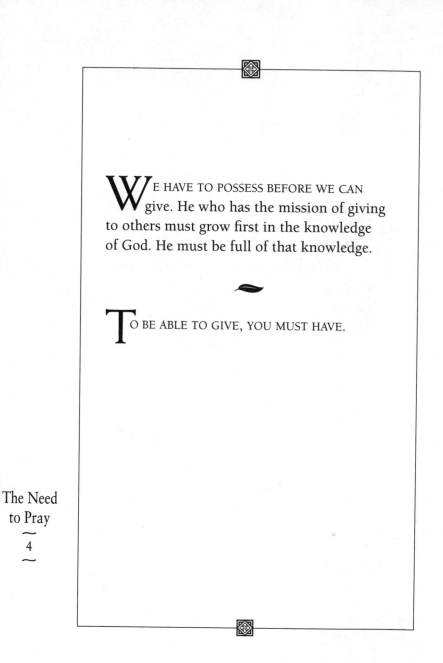

T O BE ABLE TO GIVE, YOU MUST HAVE.

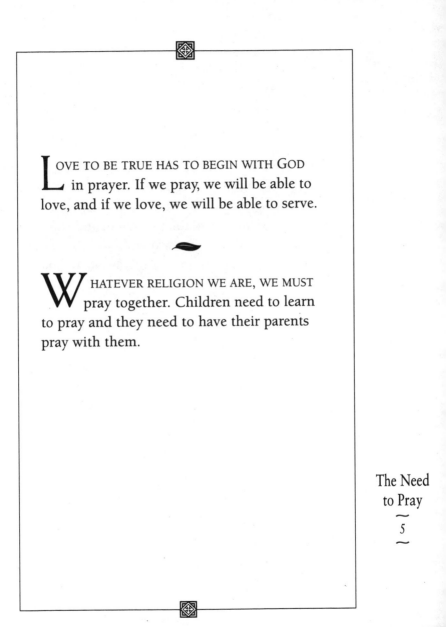

LOVE TO BE TRUE HAS TO BEGIN WITH GOD in prayer. If we pray, we will be able to love, and if we love, we will be able to serve.

WHATEVER RELIGION WE ARE, WE MUST pray together. Children need to learn to pray and they need to have their parents pray with them.

The Need
to Pray

~
5
~

I T IS EASY TO LOVE THE PEOPLE FAR AWAY.
It is not always easy to love those close to
us. It is easier to give a cup of rice to relieve
hunger than to relieve the loneliness and pain
of someone unloved in our own home. Bring
love into your own home for this is where our
love for each other must start.

I N ONE OF THE HOUSES OUR SISTERS VISITED, a woman had been dead a long time before anyone knew it, and then they found out only because her corpse had begun to rot. Her neighbors didn't even know her name.

T HERE IS MUCH SUFFERING IN THE WORLD — very much. And this material suffering is suffering from hunger, suffering from homelessness, from all kinds of diseases, but I still think the greatest suffering is being lonely, feeling unloved, just having no one.

THERE ARE DIFFERENT KINDS OF POVERTY. In India some people live and die in hunger.

But in the West you have another kind of poverty, spiritual poverty. This is far worse. People do not believe in God, do not pray. People do not care for each other. You have the poverty of people who are dissatisfied with what they have, who do not know how to suffer, who give in to despair. This poverty of heart is often more difficult to relieve and to defeat.

I REMEMBER SOME TIME AGO I VISITED A very wonderful home for old people. There were about forty there and they had everything, but they were all looking toward the door. There was not a smile on their faces, and I asked the sister in charge of them, "Sister, why are these people not smiling? Why are they looking towards the door?" And she, very beautifully, had to answer and give the truth: "It's the same every day. They are longing for someone to come and visit them." This is great poverty.

⟣

W HEN THINGS BECOME OUR MASTERS, we are very poor.

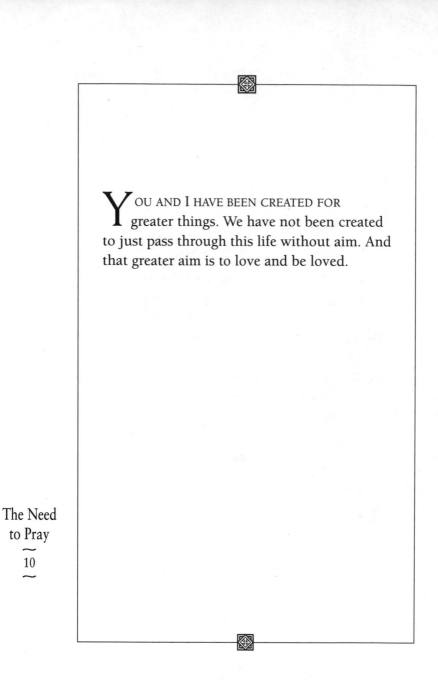

YOU AND I HAVE BEEN CREATED FOR greater things. We have not been created to just pass through this life without aim. And that greater aim is to love and be loved.

S OME CALL HIM ISHWAR, SOME CALL
Him Allah, some simply God, but we
all have to acknowledge that it is He who
made us for greater things: to love and be
loved. What matters is that we love. We
cannot love without prayer, and so whatever religion we are we must pray together.

YOU WILL FIND CALCUTTA ALL OVER THE world if you have eyes to see. The streets of Calcutta lead to every man's door. I know that you may want to make a trip to Calcutta, but it is easy to love people far away. It is not always easy to love people who live beside us. What about the ones I dislike or look down upon?

IT IS EASY TO BE PROUD AND HARSH AND selfish — so easy. But we have been created for better things.

ONCE IN A WHILE WE SHOULD ASK ourselves several questions in order to guide our actions. We should ask questions like: Do I know the poor? Do I know, in the first place, the poor in my family, those who are closest to me — people who are poor, but not because they lack bread?

There are other types of poverty just as painful because they are more intrinsic.

Perhaps what my husband or wife lacks, what my children lack, what my parents lack, is not clothes or food. Perhaps they lack love, because I do not give it to them!

WHERE DOES LOVE BEGIN?
In our own homes.
When does it begin?
When we pray together.

WE HAVE TO FEED OURSELVES.
We can die of spiritual starvation.
We must be filled continually, like a
machine. When one little thing in
the machine is not working, then
the whole machine is not working
properly.

I AM ASKED WHAT IS ONE TO DO to be sure one is following the way of salvation. I answer: "Love God. And, above all, pray."

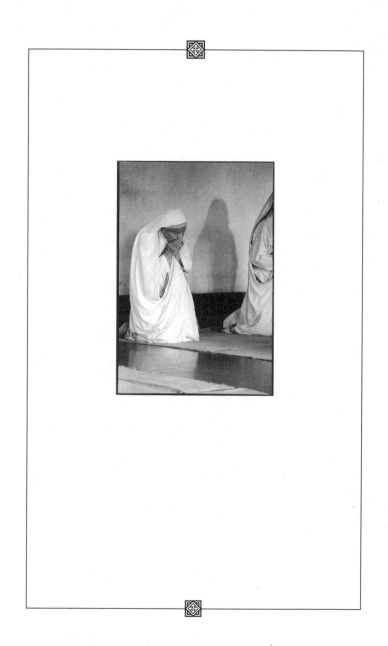

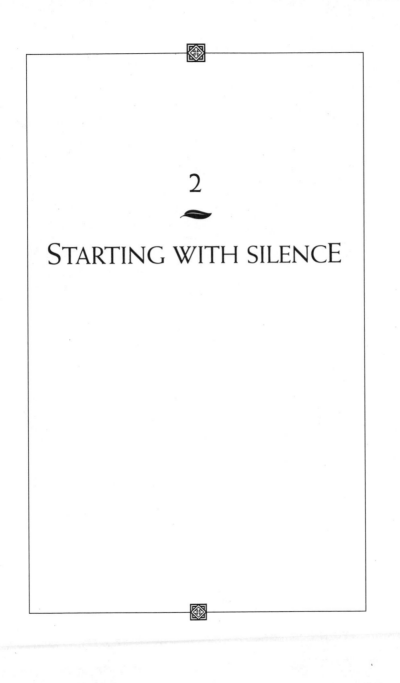

2

STARTING WITH SILENCE

I T IS VERY HARD TO PRAY IF ONE DOES not know how. We must help ourselves to learn. The most important thing is silence.

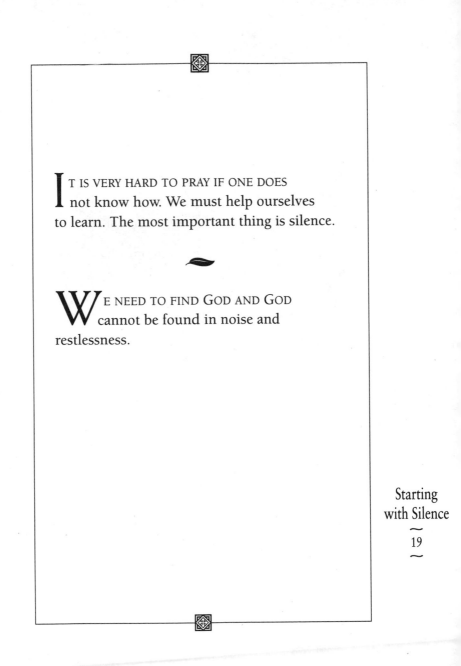

W E NEED TO FIND GOD AND GOD cannot be found in noise and restlessness.

WE CANNOT PLACE OURSELVES DIRECTLY in God's presence without imposing upon ourselves interior and exterior silence.

That is why we must accustom ourselves
to stillness of the soul,
of the eyes,
of the tongue.

T HERE IS NO LIFE OF PRAYER WITHOUT
silence.

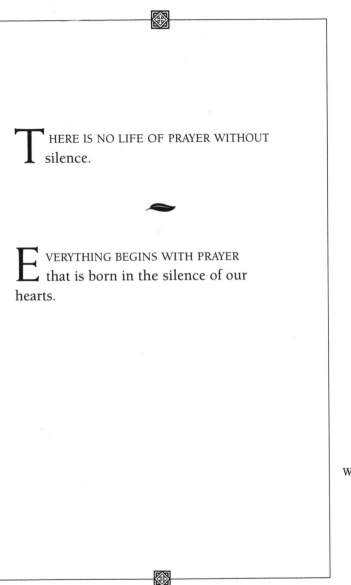

E VERYTHING BEGINS WITH PRAYER
that is born in the silence of our
hearts.

I F WE REALLY WANT TO PRAY, WE MUST first learn to listen: for in the silence of the heart God speaks.

~

S ILENCE OF THE *HEART*, NOT ONLY OF the mouth — that too is necessary.
Then you can hear God everywhere:
in the closing of the door,
in the person who needs you,
in the birds that sing,
in the flowers, the animals —
that silence which is wonder and praise.

T HE CONTEMPLATIVES AND ASCETICS
of all ages and religions have sought
God in the silence and solitude of the
desert, forest, and mountain.

W E TOO ARE CALLED TO WITHDRAW
at certain intervals into deeper
silence and aloneness with God, together
as a community as well as personally. To
be alone with him, not with our books,
thoughts, and memories but completely
stripped of everything, to dwell lovingly
in his presence — silent, empty, expec-
tant, and motionless.

LISTEN IN SILENCE, BECAUSE IF YOUR HEART is full of other things you cannot hear the voice of God. But when you have listened to the voice of God in the stillness of your heart, then your heart is filled with God. This will need much sacrifice, but if we really mean to pray and want to pray we must be ready to do it now.

T O FOSTER AND MAINTAIN A PRAYERFUL atmosphere of exterior silence we shall

~ respect certain times and places of more strict silence

~ move about and work prayerfully, quietly and gently

~ avoid at all costs all unnecessary speaking and notice

~ speak, when we have to, softly, gently, saying just what is necessary

~ look forward to profound silence as a holy and precious time, a withdrawal into the living silence of God.

W E NEED SILENCE TO BE ALONE WITH God, to speak to him, to listen to him, to ponder his words deep in our hearts. We need to be alone with God in silence to be renewed and to be transformed. Silence gives us a new outlook on life. In it we are filled with the grace of God himself, which makes us do all things with joy.

I F WE ARE CAREFUL OF SILENCE
it will be easy to pray.
There is so much talk,
so much repetition,
so much carrying on
of tales in words and in writing.
Our prayer life suffers so much
because our hearts are not silent.

LOOKING AT YOUR EYES
I can tell whether there is peace
in your heart or not.

We see people radiating joy,
and in their eyes you can see purity.
If we want our minds to have silence,
keep a silence of the eyes.
Use your two eyes to help you to
pray better.

MAN NEEDS SILENCE.

To be alone or together
looking for God in silence.

There it is that we accumulate the
inward power which we distribute in
action, put in the smallest duty and spend
in the severest hardships that befall us.

Silence came before creation,
and the heavens were spread
without a word.

I NTERIOR SILENCE IS VERY DIFFICULT
but we must make the effort. In silence
we will find new energy and true unity.
The energy of God will be ours to do all
things well.

T HESE ARE ONLY THE FIRST STEPS
toward prayer, but if we never
make the first step with determination,
we will not reach the last one:
the presence of God.

I F YOU SINCERELY WANT TO LEARN TO PRAY:
keep silence.

3

LIKE A LITTLE CHILD

M Y SECRET IS A VERY SIMPLE ONE:
I pray.

P RAYER IS SIMPLY TALKING TO GOD.
He speaks to us: we listen.
We speak to him: he listens.
A two-way process:
speaking and listening.

That is really prayer.
Both sides listening
and both sides speaking.

S TART AND END THE DAY WITH PRAYER.
Come to God as a child.
If you find it hard to pray you can say,
"Come Holy Spirit,
guide me, protect me,
clear out my mind
so that I can pray."

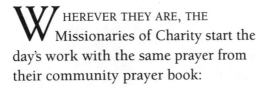

WHEREVER THEY ARE, THE Missionaries of Charity start the day's work with the same prayer from their community prayer book:

Dear Lord, the Great Healer,
I kneel before you, since every
perfect gift must come from you.
I pray, give skill to my hands,
clear vision to my mind,
kindness and meekness to my heart.
Give me singleness of purpose,
strength to lift up a part of the
burden of my suffering fellowmen,
and a realization of the privilege
that is mine. Take from my heart
all guile and worldliness, that with the
simple faith of a child, I may rely on you.
Amen.

HOW DO YOU PRAY?
You should go to God like a little child. A child has no difficulty expressing his mind in simple words that say so much.

If a child is not yet spoiled and has not yet learned to tell lies, he will tell everything. This is what I mean by being childlike.

H OW DO WE LEARN TO PRAY?
By praying. It is very hard to pray
if one does not know how. We must help
ourselves to learn. Pray with absolute
trust in God's loving care for you and
let him fill you with joy that you may
preach without preaching.

Y OU CAN PRAY ANYTIME, ANYWHERE.
You do not have to be in a chapel
or a church.

L OVE TO PRAY — FEEL THE NEED TO PRAY
often during the day and take the
trouble to pray. If you want to pray better,
you must pray more.

T HE MORE YOU PRAY, THE EASIER IT
becomes. The easier it becomes,
the more you'll pray.

Y OU CAN PRAY WHILE YOU WORK.
Work doesn't stop prayer and prayer
doesn't stop work. It requires only that
small raising of the mind to him:
"I love you God,
I trust you,
I believe in you,
I need you now."
Small things like that.
They are wonderful prayers.

OFTEN, UNDER THE PRETEXT OF HUMILITY,
of trust, of abandonment, we can
forget to use the strength of our will.
Everything depends on these words:
"I will" or "I will not."
And into the expression "I will"
I must put all my energy.

WE MUST KNOW THE MEANING OF
the prayers we say and feel the
sweetness of each word to make these
prayers of great profit; we must sometimes
meditate on them and often during the
day find our rest in them.

Y OU CAN SAY, "My Lord, I love You."
"My God, I am sorry."
"My God, I believe in You."
"My God, I trust You."
"Help us to love one another
as You love us."

Y OU CAN PRAY FOR THE WORKS OF
others and help them. For example,
in our community there are second self
helpers who offer their prayers for a sister
who needs the strength to carry on her
active work. And we also have the contemplative sisters and brothers, who pray
for us all the time.

"I KEPT THE LORD EVER BEFORE MY EYES because he is ever at my right hand that I may not slip," says the psalmist. God is within me with a more intimate presence than that whereby I am in myself: in him we live and move and have our being. It is he who gives life to all, that gives power and being to all that exists. But for his sustaining presence, all things would cease to be and fall back into nothingness.

C ONSIDER THAT YOU ARE IN GOD, surrounded and encompassed by God, swimming in God.

W E NEED TO HELP EACH OTHER
in our prayers. Let us free our minds.
Let's not pray long, drawn-out prayers, but
let's pray short ones full of love. Let us pray
on behalf of those who do not pray. Let us
remember, if we want to be able to love, we
must be able to pray!

I T IS NOW SEVEN HUNDRED AND FIFTY
years since St. Francis of Assisi composed
the following prayer for himself and for those
whom he taught to love God:

Lord, make me an instrument of your peace.
Where there is hatred, let me sow love.
Where there is injury, let me sow pardon.
Where there is friction, let me sow union.
Where there is error, let me sow truth.
Where there is doubt, let me sow faith.
Where there is despair, let me sow hope.
Where there is darkness, let me sow light.
Where there is sadness, let me sow joy.

O Divine Master, grant that I may not so
much seek
To be consoled as to console,
To be understood as to understand,
To be loved as to love,
For it is in giving that we receive.
It is in pardoning that we are pardoned.
It is in dying that we are born to eternal life.

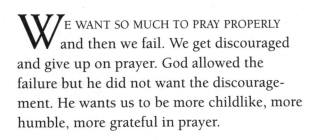

WE WANT SO MUCH TO PRAY PROPERLY and then we fail. We get discouraged and give up on prayer. God allowed the failure but he did not want the discouragement. He wants us to be more childlike, more humble, more grateful in prayer.

TRY SPEAKING DIRECTLY TO GOD.
Just speak. Tell him everything, talk to him. He is our father, he is father to us all whatever religion we are. We have to put our trust in him and love him, believe in him, work for him. And if we pray, we will get all the answers we need.

LET GOD USE YOU WITHOUT CONSULTING you: "You, Lord, only You, all for You; make use of me."

O NE OF MY FAVORITE DEVOTIONAL SONGS is called *Only a Shadow*. Its verses run like this:

The love I have for you, my Lord
Is only a shadow of your love for me,
Your deep abiding love.
My own belief in you, my Lord,
Is only a shadow of your faith in me,
Your deep and trusting faith.
My life is in your hands.
My love for you will grow, my Lord.
Your light in me will shine.
The dream I have today, my Lord,
Is only a shadow of your dream for me,
If I but follow you.
The joy I feel today, my Lord,
Is only a shadow of your joys for me,
Only a shadow of all that will be
When we meet face to face.

T HERE ARE SOME PEOPLE WHO, IN order not to pray, use as an excuse the fact that life is so hectic that it prevents them from praying.

This cannot be.

Prayer does not demand that we interrupt our work, but that we continue working as if it were a prayer.

It is not necessary to always be meditating, nor to consciously experience the sensation that we are talking to God, no matter how nice this would be. What matters is being with him, living in him, in his will.

GOD IS PURITY HIMSELF; NOTHING IMPURE can come before him, but I don't think God can hate, because God is love and God loves us in spite of our misery.

God loves because he is love, but impurity is an obstacle to seeing God.

OUR SOULS SHOULD BE LIKE A transparent crystal through which God can be perceived.

～

OUR CRYSTAL IS SOMETIMES COVERED with dirt and dust. To remove this dust we carry out an examination of our conscience in order to obtain a clean heart. God will help us to remove that dust, as long as we allow him to: if that is our will, his will comes about.

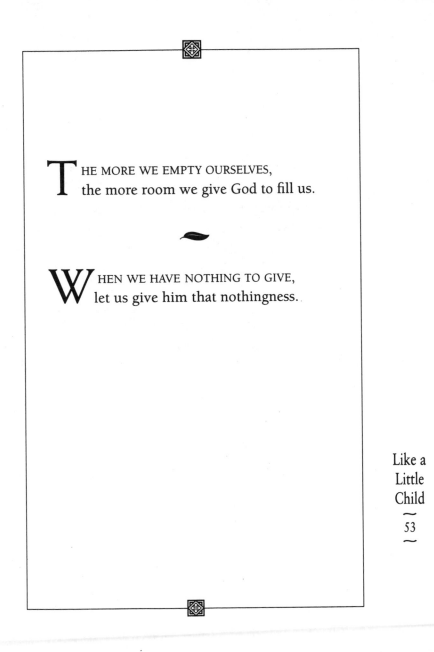

T HE MORE WE EMPTY OURSELVES,
the more room we give God to fill us.

W HEN WE HAVE NOTHING TO GIVE,
let us give him that nothingness.

R ICHES, MATERIAL OR SPIRITUAL, CAN
suffocate you if they are not used in
the right way. Remain as "empty" as possible,
so that God can fill you.

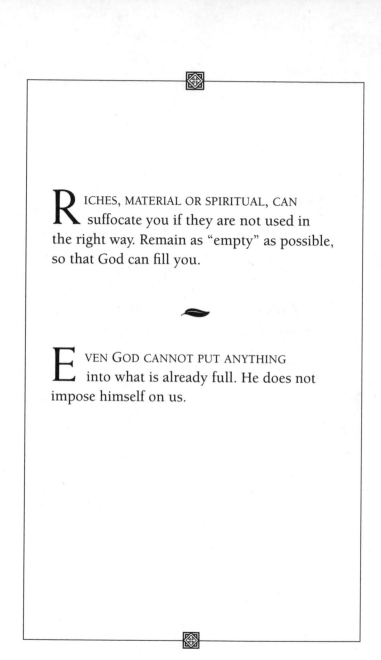

E VEN GOD CANNOT PUT ANYTHING
into what is already full. He does not
impose himself on us.

I T IS NOT HOW MUCH WE REALLY HAVE
to give but how empty we are — so that
we can receive fully in our life. Take away
your eyes from yourself and rejoice that you
have nothing — that you are nothing — that
you can do nothing.

W E HAVE TO PRAY ON BEHALF OF
those who do not pray.

W E SHOULD BE PROFESSIONALS IN
prayer.

L OVE TO PRAY. FEEL OFTEN DURING
the day the need for prayer and take
trouble to pray. God is always speaking to us.
Listen to him.

R ECREATION IS A MEANS TO PRAY BETTER.
Relaxation sweeps away the cobwebs
of the mind.

W HEN YOU PRAY, GIVE THANKS to God for all his gifts because everything is his and a gift from him.

◄

Y OUR SOUL IS A GIFT OF GOD.

A S LONG AS WE DO NOT MAKE THE best effort we are capable of, we cannot feel discouraged by our failures. We cannot claim any successes either. We should give God all the credit and be extremely sincere when we do so.

B E SINCERE IN YOUR PRAYERS. Do you pray your prayers? Do you know how to pray? Do you love to pray? Sincerity is nothing but humility and you acquire humility only by accepting humiliations.

ALL THAT HAS BEEN SAID ABOUT HUMILITY is not enough to teach you humility. All that you have read about humility is not enough to teach you humility. You learn humility only by accepting humiliations. And you will meet humiliation all through your lives.

THE GREATEST HUMILIATION IS TO KNOW that you are nothing. This you come to know when you face God in prayer. When you come face to face with God, you cannot but know that you are nothing, that you have nothing.

I F WE REALLY FULLY BELONG TO GOD,
then we must be at his disposal and
we must trust in him. We must never be
preoccupied with the future. There is no
reason to be so. God is there.

Y ESTERDAY IS GONE.
Tomorrow has not yet come.
We have only today.
Let us begin.

D ON'T SEARCH FOR GOD IN FAR LANDS —
he is not there. He is close to you. He
is with you. Just keep the lamp burning and
you will always see him. Watch and pray.
Keep kindling the lamp and you will see his
love and you will see how sweet is the Lord
you love.

T ODAY, MORE THAN EVER, WE NEED
to pray for the light to know the will of
God, for the love to accept the will of God,
for the way to do the will of God.

P RAY LOVINGLY LIKE CHILDREN,
with an earnest desire to love much
and make loved the love that is not loved.

Let us thank God for all his love for us, in so
many ways and in so many places.

M AY GOD GIVE US ALL OPENNESS TO
ways leading beyond our own selves.

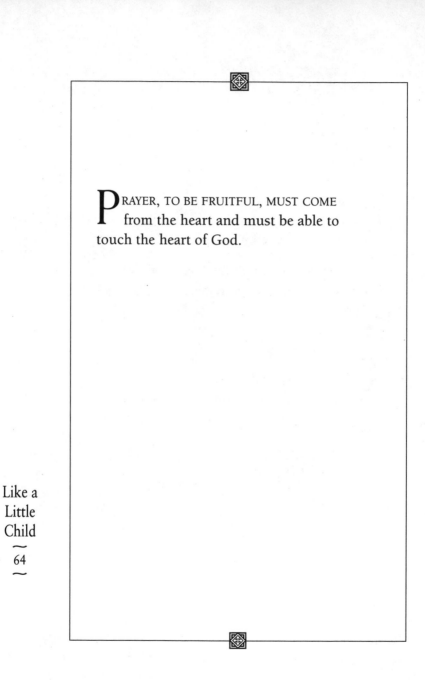

Prayer, to be fruitful, must come from the heart and must be able to touch the heart of God.

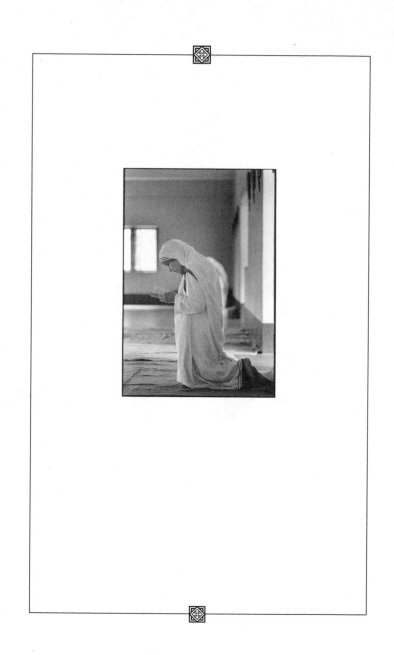

4

OPENING YOUR HEART

OPEN YOUR HEARTS
to the love of God
which he will give you.
He loves you with tenderness.
And he will give you not to keep
but to share.

OUR PRAYERS SHOULD BE BURNING words coming forth from the furnace of hearts filled with love. In your prayers, speak to God with great reverence and confidence.

D O NOT DRAG BEHIND OR RUN AHEAD;
do not shout or keep silent,
but devoutly, with great sweetness,
with natural simplicity,
without any affectation,
offer your praise to God
with the whole of your heart and soul.

WE OUGHT EVERY DAY TO RENEW
our resolution and to rouse
ourselves to fervor, as if it were the first
day of our conversion, saying,
"Help me, Lord God,
in my good resolve
and in thy holy service,
and give me grace this very day
really and truly to begin,
for what I have done till now is nothing."

THE PRAYER THAT COMES FROM THE mind and heart and which we do not read in books is called mental prayer. In vocal prayer we speak to God; in mental prayer he speaks to us. It is then that God pours himself into us.

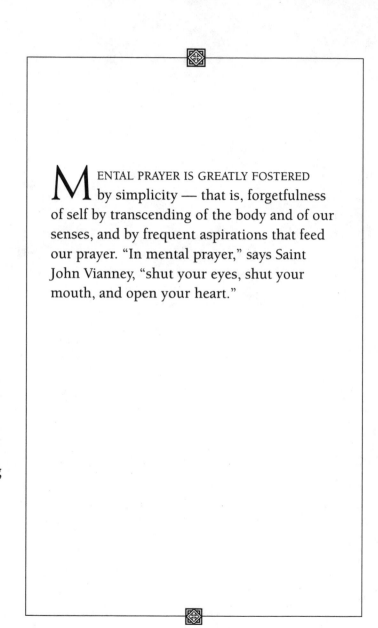

MENTAL PRAYER IS GREATLY FOSTERED by simplicity — that is, forgetfulness of self by transcending of the body and of our senses, and by frequent aspirations that feed our prayer. "In mental prayer," says Saint John Vianney, "shut your eyes, shut your mouth, and open your heart."

P RAYER ENLARGES THE HEART UNTIL
it is capable of containing God's gift of
himself. Ask and seek and your heart will
grow big enough to receive him and keep
him as your own.

O FFER TO GOD EVERY WORD YOU SAY,
every movement you make.
We must more and more
fall in love with God.

W E NEED PRAYERS IN ORDER TO BETTER
carry out the work of God, and so that
in every moment we may know how to be
completely available to him.

We should make every effort
to walk in the presence of God,
to see God in all the persons we meet,
to live our prayer throughout the day.

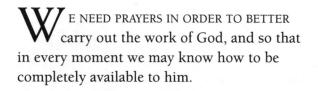

W E MUST PRAY PERSEVERINGLY
and with great love.

L OVE IS A FRUIT IN SEASON AT ALL TIMES
and within the reach of every hand.
Anyone may gather it and no limit is set.
Everyone can reach this love through
meditation,
the spirit of prayer and sacrifice,
by an intense inner life.

Do we really live this life?

L OVING SHOULD BE AS NORMAL TO US
as living and breathing, day after day
until our death.

A M I A DARK LIGHT? A FALSE LIGHT?
A bulb without the connection,
therefore shedding no radiance?

Put your heart into being a bright light.

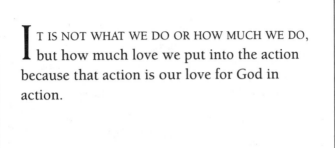

I T IS NOT WHAT WE DO OR HOW MUCH WE DO, but how much love we put into the action because that action is our love for God in action.

G OD SPEAKS IN THE SILENCE
of our heart, and we listen.
And then we speak to God from the
fullness of our heart, and God listens.

⟡

E VEN WHEN WE SIN OR MAKE A MISTAKE,
let's allow that to help us grow closer
to God. Let's tell him humbly, "I know I
shouldn't have done this, but even this failure
I offer to you."

O UR WORDS ARE USELESS UNLESS
they come from the bottom of the
heart.

G IVE YOURSELF FULLY TO GOD.
He will use you to accomplish
great things on the condition
that you believe much more
in his love than in your weakness.

I S MY HEART SO CLEAN THAT I CAN SEE
the face of God in my brother, my sister
who is that black one, that white one, that
naked one, that one suffering from leprosy,
that dying one?

And this is what we must pray for.

G OD DWELLS IN US.
That's what gives him a beautiful power.
It doesn't matter where you are as long
as you are clean of heart. Clean of heart means
openness, that complete freedom,
that detachment that allows you to love God
without hindrance, without obstacles.

E VERY NIGHT BEFORE YOU GO TO BED
you must make an examination of
conscience (because you don't know if you
will be alive in the morning!). Whatever is
troubling you, or whatever wrong you may
have done, you need to repair it. For example,
if you have stolen something, then try to give
it back.

I F YOU HAVE HURT SOMEBODY,
try to make up to that person;
do it directly. If you cannot make up like that,
at least then make up with God by saying,
"I'm very sorry." This is important because
just as we have acts of love, we also must
have acts of contrition. You could say,
"Lord, I'm sorry for having offended you
and I promise you I will try not to offend
you again."

I T FEELS GOOD TO BE FREE OF BURDENS, to have a clean heart. Remember that God is merciful, he is the merciful father to us all. We are his children and he will forgive and forget if we remember to do so.

E XAMINE YOUR HEART FIRST, THOUGH, to see if there is any lack of forgiveness of others still inside, because how can we ask God for forgiveness if we cannot forgive others?

P EOPLE ASK ME WHAT ADVICE I HAVE FOR
a married couple struggling in their
relationship. I always answer "Pray and
forgive"; and to young people who come
from violent homes, "Pray and forgive"; and
to the single mother with no family support,
"Pray and forgive."

REMEMBER, IF YOU TRULY REPENT,
if you really mean it with a clean heart,
you will be absolved in God's eyes. He will
forgive you if you truly confess. So pray to be
able to forgive those who have hurt you or
whom you don't like, and forgive as you have
been forgiven.

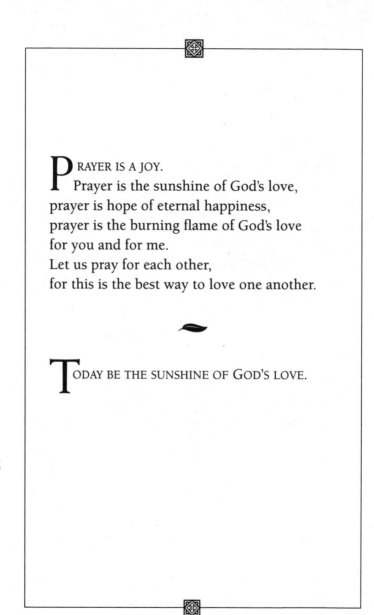

P RAYER IS A JOY.
  Prayer is the sunshine of God's love,
prayer is hope of eternal happiness,
prayer is the burning flame of God's love
for you and for me.
Let us pray for each other,
for this is the best way to love one another.

T ODAY BE THE SUNSHINE OF GOD'S LOVE.

G OD IS STILL LOVE,
he is still loving the world.
Today God loves the world so much
that he gives you and he gives me to love
the world, to be his love and compassion.

Y OU MAY BE EXHAUSTED WITH WORK,
even kill yourself, but unless your work
is interwoven with love, it is useless.

W E MUST ALL FILL OUR HEARTS WITH
great love. Don't imagine that love, to
be true and burning, must be extraordinary.

G OD LOVES EACH ONE OF US
with a most tender and personal love.
His longing for me is dearer than my
longing for him.

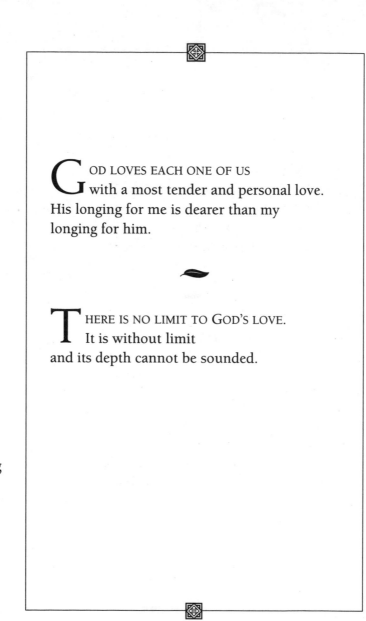

T HERE IS NO LIMIT TO GOD'S LOVE.
It is without limit
and its depth cannot be sounded.

T HE BEST WAY TO SHOW YOUR GRATITUDE to God and people is to accept everything with joy. A joyful heart is the normal result of a heart burning with love.

I T IS SO EASY TO BE PROUD, HARSH, MOODY and selfish, but we have been created for greater things; why stoop down to things that will spoil the beauty of our hearts?

IN THE SILENCE OF THE HEART GOD SPEAKS.

What does God say to us? He says:
"I have called you by your name, you are mine;
water will not drown you,
fire will not burn you,
I will give up nations for you,
you are precious to me, I love you.
Even if a mother could forget her child,
I will not forget you.
I have carved you in the palm of my hand."

W E CANNOT SPEAK UNLESS WE HAVE
listened, unless we have made our
connection with God. From the fullness of
the heart, the mouth will speak, the mind
will think.

P RAYER ENLARGES THE HEART UNTIL
it is capable of containing God's gift of
himself.

J UST ONCE, LET THE LOVE OF GOD
take entire and absolute possession of
your heart; let it become to your heart like a
second nature; let your heart suffer nothing
contrary to enter; let it apply itself continually
to increase this love of God by seeking to
please him in all things and refusing him
nothing; let it accept as from his hand
everything that happens to it; let it have a
firm determination never to commit any fault
deliberately and knowingly or, if it should
fail, to be humbled and to rise up again
at once — and such a heart will pray
continually.

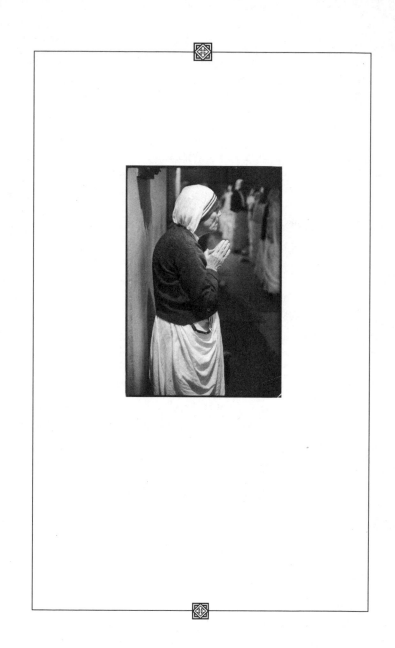

5

ENDING IN SILENCE

S OULS OF PRAYER ARE SOULS OF GREAT
silence.

S ILENCE IS THE BEAUTIFUL FRUIT OF PRAYER.
We must learn not only the silence
of the mouth but also
the silence of the heart,
of the eyes,
of the ears
and of the mind,
which I call the five silences.

G OD IS THE FRIEND OF SILENCE.
See how nature — trees, flowers, grass
— grows in silence.
See the stars,
the moon,
and the sun,
how they move in silence.

I N THAT SILENCE, HE WILL LISTEN TO US;
there he will speak to our soul,
and there we will hear his voice.

T HE FRUIT OF SILENCE IS FAITH.
The fruit of faith is prayer.
The fruit of prayer is love.
The fruit of love is service.
And the fruit of service is silence.

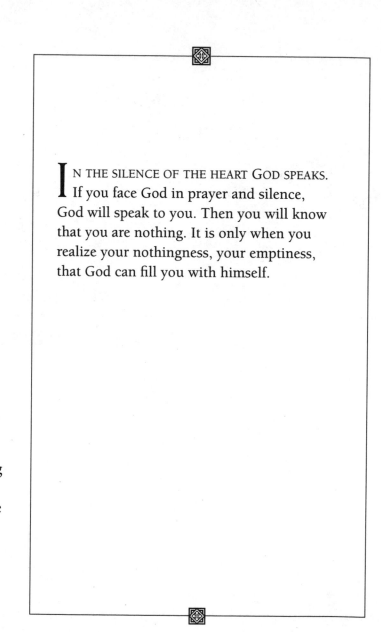

I N THE SILENCE OF THE HEART GOD SPEAKS.
If you face God in prayer and silence,
God will speak to you. Then you will know
that you are nothing. It is only when you
realize your nothingness, your emptiness,
that God can fill you with himself.

S ILENCE GIVES US A NEW WAY OF LOOKING
at everything. We need this silence in
order to touch souls.

G OD IS THE FRIEND OF SILENCE.
His language is silence.
"Be still and know that I am God."

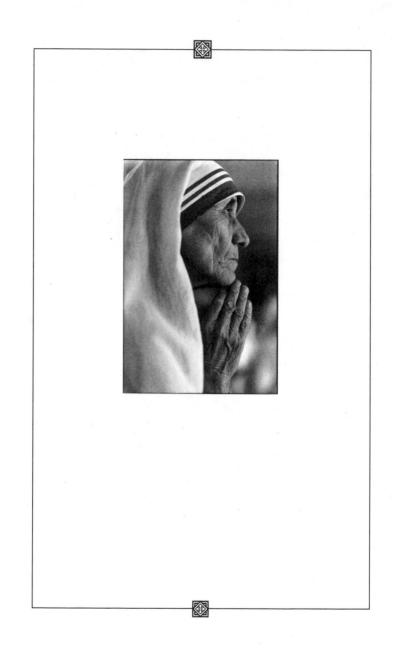

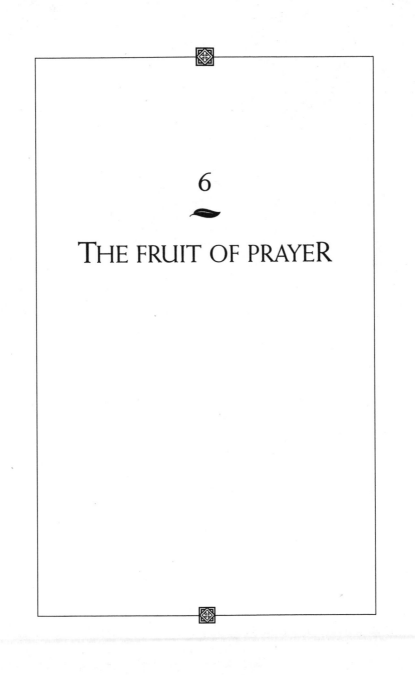

6

THE FRUIT OF PRAYER

T HE MORE WE RECEIVE IN SILENT PRAYER,
the more we can give in our active life.

T HE ESSENTIAL THING IS NOT WHAT WE SAY,
but what God says to us and through us.

All our words will be useless unless they
come from within.

Y OU CAN DO WHAT I CAN'T DO.
I can do what you can't do.
Together we can do something
beautiful for God.

G OD DOES NOT DEMAND
that I be successful.
God demands that I be faithful.

When facing God, results are not important.
Faithfulness is what is important.

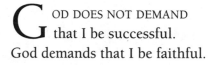

W E DO NOT STRIVE FOR SPECTACULAR
actions. What counts is the gift of
yourself, the degree of love you put into
each of your deeds.

W E CAN DO NO GREAT THINGS —
only small things with great love.

T HE FRUIT OF PRAYER IS A DEEPENING OF FAITH.

B E FAITHFUL IN SMALL THINGS
because it is in them that your
strength lies.

P RAYER FEEDS THE SOUL —
as blood is to the body,
prayer is to the soul —
and it brings you closer to God.

W HEN YOU BECOME FULL OF GOD,
you will do all your work well,
all of it wholeheartedly.
And when you are full of God,
you will do everything well.
This you can do only if you pray,
if you know how to pray,
if you love prayer,
and if you pray well.

T HE MORE I GO AROUND, THE BETTER
I understand how very necessary it is
for us to pray the work, to make the work
our love for God in action.

G OD MAY ALLOW EVERYTHING
to go upside down in the hands of a
very talented and capable person. Unless the
work is interwoven with love, it is useless.

L OVE IS NOT SOMETHING THAT FOSSILIZES,
  but something that lives. Works of love,
and declaring love, is the way to peace.
And where does this love begin?
Right in our own hearts.
We must know that we have been
created for greater things,
not just to be a number in the world,
not just to go for diplomas and degrees,
this work and that work.

We have been created in order to love
and be loved.

I F WE NEGLECT PRAYER AND IF THE BRANCH IS
not connected with the vine, it will die.
That connecting of the branch to the vine
is prayer. If that connection is there
then love is there, then joy is there,
and we will be the sunshine of God's love,
the hope of eternal happiness,
the flame of burning love.

T HIS IS THE TRUE REASON FOR OUR
existence: to be the sunshine of God's
love, to be the hope of eternal happiness.
That's all.

T HE FRUIT OF PRAYER IS A CLEAN HEART
and a clean heart is free to love.

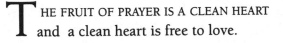

W HEN YOU HAVE A CLEAN HEART
it means you are open and honest
with God, you are not hiding anything from
him, and this lets him take what he wants
from you.

THE ENERGY OF GOD WILL BE OURS
to do all things well, and so will the
unity of our thoughts with his thoughts,
the unity of our prayers with his prayers,
the unity of our actions with his actions,
of our life with his life.
Unity is the fruit of prayer,
of humility, of love.

THE VALUE OF OUR ACTIONS
corresponds exactly to the value
of the prayer we make.

N EVER THINK THAT A SMALL ACTION DONE
to your neighbor is not worth much.
It is not how much we do that is pleasing to
God, but how much love we put into the
doing.

Make sure you know your neighbor,
for that knowledge will lead you to great love
and love to personal service.

W E IMPATIENTLY AWAIT GOD'S PARADISE,
but we have in our hands the power
to be in paradise right here and now.
Being happy with God means this:
to love as he loves,
to help as he helps,
to give as he gives,
to serve as he serves.

L OVE ACCEPTS ALL AND GIVES ALL.
Love should be as natural as living
and breathing.

I N THE SILENCE OF THE HEART,
God speaks and you have to listen.
Then in the fullness of your heart,
because it is full of God,
full of love,
full of compassion,
full of faith,
your mouth will speak.

Y OU MAY BE WRITING, AND THE FULLNESS
of your heart will come to your hand also.
Your heart may speak through writing.
Your heart may speak through your eyes also.
You know that when you look at people they
must be able to see God in your eyes.
If you get distracted and worldly,
then they will not be able to see God like that.
The fullness of our heart is expressed
in our eyes, in our touch, in what we write,
in what we say, in the way we walk,
the way we receive, the way we need.
That is the fullness of our heart
expressing itself in many different ways.

WE DO NOT ROAM, BUT WE CULTIVATE
the vagabond spirit of abandonment.
We have nothing to live on,
yet we live splendidly;
nothing to walk on,
yet we walk fearlessly;
nothing to lean on,
but yet we lean on God confidently;
for we are his own and
he is our provident father.

WE ARE CALLED UPON NOT TO BE
successful, but to be faithful.

WE GET SO MANY VISITORS EVERY DAY at Mother House in Calcutta. When I meet them I give each one my "business card." On it is written: *The fruit of prayer is faith; The fruit of faith is love; The fruit of love is service; The fruit of service is peace.*

This is very good "business"!

At the Home for the Dying in Kalighat, a visitor wondered at the peace that pervaded everywhere. I said simply: "God is here. Castes and creeds mean nothing. It does not matter that they are not of my faith."

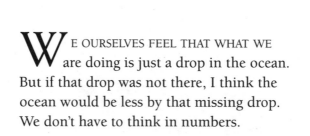

W E OURSELVES FEEL THAT WHAT WE
are doing is just a drop in the ocean.
But if that drop was not there, I think the
ocean would be less by that missing drop.
We don't have to think in numbers.

We can only love one person at a time,
serve one person at a time.

W HEREVER GOD HAS PUT YOU,
that is your vocation.
It is not what we do but how
much love we put into it.

~

T O THE CAST OF A MUSICAL PERFORMANCE
in Calcutta, I said: "Your work and our
work complete each other. What we are doing
is needed in the world as never before. You
are giving them joy by your action and we are
doing the same by service. And it is the same
action whether you are singing and dancing
and we are rubbing and scrubbing. You are
filling the world with love God has given you.

The
Fruit of
Prayer
~
125
~

J OY SHOWS FROM THE EYES,
it appears when one speaks and walks.
It cannot be kept closed inside us.
It reacts outside. When people find in
your eyes that habitual happiness,
they will understand that they are
the beloved children of God.

W E ARE TALKING ABOUT THE JOY
that comes from union with God,
from living in his presence, because
living in his presence fills us with joy.

When I speak of joy, I do not identify it
with loud laughter or with noise.
This is not true happiness.
Sometimes it hides other things.

When I speak of happiness,
I refer to an inner and deep peace,
which shows itself in our eyes, on our faces,
in our attitudes, in our gestures,
in our promptness.

T HAT IS WHAT I SEE HAPPENING:
people coming to meet each other
because of their need for God.
The wonderful thing about it is that
there is a religious atmosphere;
they all speak about God.

This is a great experience for me.
I feel that to bring all these people together
to talk about God is really wonderful.
A new hope for the world.

T HERE IS A TREMENDOUS STRENGTH
that is growing in the world through this
continual sharing, praying together, suffering
together and working together.

W E DO NOTHING. HE DOES EVERYTHING.
All glory must be returned to him.

God has not called me to be successful.
He called me to be faithful.

ONE DAY IN CALCUTTA A MAN CAME WITH a prescription and said, "My only child is dying and this medicine can be brought only from outside of India." Just at that time, while we were still talking, a man came with a basket of medicine. Right on the top of that basket, there was this medicine.

If it had been inside, I would not have seen it. If he had come before, or if he had come afterward, I could not have seen it. But just at that time, out of the millions and millions of children in the world, God in his tenderness was concerned with this little child of the slums of Calcutta enough to send, just at that time, that amount of medicine to save that child.

I praise the tenderness and the love of God, because every little one, in a poor family or a rich family, is a child of God, created by the Creator of all things.

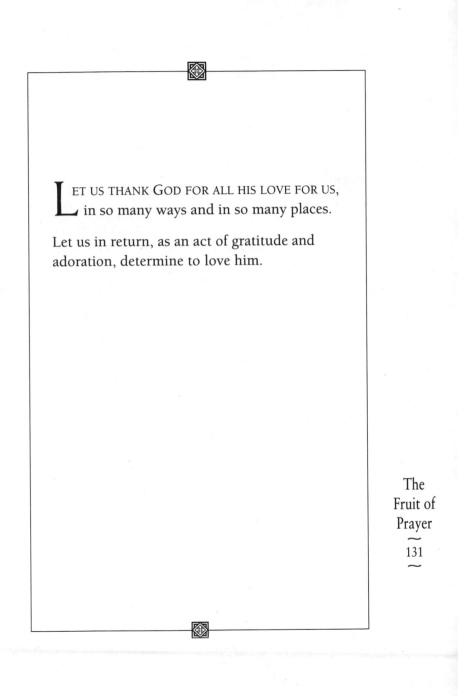

L ET US THANK GOD FOR ALL HIS LOVE FOR US, in so many ways and in so many places.

Let us in return, as an act of gratitude and adoration, determine to love him.

The
Fruit of
Prayer
~
131
~

H OLINESS IS NOT A LUXURY FOR THE FEW;
it is not just for some people.
It is meant for you and for me, for all of us.
It is a simple duty, because if we learn to love,
we learn to be holy.

W E ALL HAVE MUCH TO GIVE,
to share, to contribute wherever
we find ourselves to be living.

Holiness starts in the home, by loving God
and those around us for his sake.

T OTAL SURRENDER TO GOD MUST COME
in small details just as it comes in big
details. It's nothing but that single word,
"Yes, I accept whatever you give,
and I give whatever you take."
And this is just a simple way for us to be holy.

W E MUST NOT CREATE DIFFICULTIES IN
our own minds. To be holy doesn't
mean to do extraordinary things, to
understand big things, but it is a simple
acceptance, because I have given myself to
God, because I belong to him — my total
surrender. He could put me here. He could
put me there. He can use me. He cannot use
me. It doesn't matter because I belong so
totally to him that he can do just what he
wants to do with me.

M AKE SURE THAT YOU LET GOD'S GRACE
work in your souls by accepting
whatever he gives you, and giving him
whatever he takes from you. True holiness
consists in doing God's will with a smile.

O UR PROGRESS IN HOLINESS DEPENDS
on God and on ourselves — on God's
grace and on our will to be holy. We must have
a real living determination to reach holiness.

W E MUST NOT ATTEMPT TO CONTROL
God's actions. We must not count the
stages in the journey he would have us make.
We must not desire a clear perception of our
advance along the road, nor know precisely
where we are on the way of holiness.

B ECOME HOLY. EACH ONE OF US
has a capacity to become holy
and the way to holiness is prayer.

W E TREAT ALL PEOPLE AS CHILDREN OF
God. They are our brothers and sisters.
We show great respect to them. Our work is
to encourage these people, Christians as well
as non-Christians, to do works of love.
Every work of love done with a full heart
brings people closer to God.

E VERY HUMAN BEING COMES
    from the hand of God, and we all know
what is the love of God for us.

God has his own ways and means to work in
the hearts of men and we do not know how
close they are to him but by their actions we
will always know whether they are at this
disposal or not. Whether you are a Hindu, a
Moslem or a Christian, how you
live your life is the proof that you are fully
his or not.

L OVING MUST BE AS NORMAL TO US
   as living and breathing,
day after day until our death.
To understand this and practice it
we need much prayer,
the kind that unites us with God
and overflows continually upon others.

O UR WORKS OF CHARITY ARE NOTHING
   but the overflow of our love of God
from within. Therefore, the one who is most
united to him loves her neighbor most.

L ET NO ONE GLORY IN THEIR SUCCESS
but refer all to God in
deepest thankfulness; on the other hand,
no failure should dishearten them
as long as they have done their best.
God sees only our love.
God will not ask how many
books we have read,
how many miracles we have worked,
but whether we have done our best
for the love of him.
Have we played well?
Slept well?
Eaten well?
Nothing is small for God.

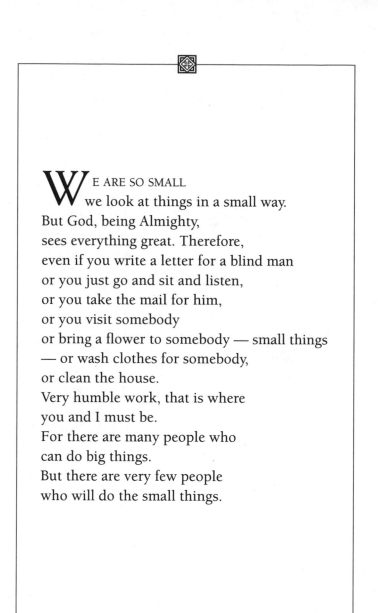

WE ARE SO SMALL
we look at things in a small way.
But God, being Almighty,
sees everything great. Therefore,
even if you write a letter for a blind man
or you just go and sit and listen,
or you take the mail for him,
or you visit somebody
or bring a flower to somebody — small things
— or wash clothes for somebody,
or clean the house.
Very humble work, that is where
you and I must be.
For there are many people who
can do big things.
But there are very few people
who will do the small things.

I T IS SO BEAUTIFUL THAT WE
complete each other!
What we are doing in the slums,
maybe you cannot do.
What you are doing in the level
where you are called — in your family life,
in your college life, in your work —
we cannot do.
But you and we together
are doing something beautiful for God.

O FTEN YOU SEE SMALL AND BIG WIRES,
new and old, cheap and expensive
electric cables. Alone they are useless,
and until the current passes through them
there will be no light. The wire is you and me.
The current is God.

W E HAVE THE POWER
to let the current pass through us
and use us to produce the light of the world
or we can refuse to be used
and allow the darkness to spread.

I F YOU HAVE LEARNED HOW TO PRAY,
then I am not afraid for you.
If you know how to pray,
then you will love prayer —
and if you love to pray,
then you will pray.
Knowledge will lead to love
and love to service.

A MONG YOURSELVES YOU CAN SHARE
your own experience of your need
to pray, and how you found prayer, and what
the fruit of prayer has been in your own lives.

L ET US SPREAD THE GOOD NEWS
that prayer is our strength.

Retreat Resources

Mother Teresa advocates taking periods of time away from one's regular routine, even one's usual spiritual routine, to develop and renew a life of prayer. Perhaps the best place to begin looking for retreats is by asking local friends, family members, spiritual advisors, or trusted community leaders what ones they may be able to suggest. (Be creative and gently persistent on this front! Knock, and eventually the right door will be opened.)

While it always makes sense to aim to take the journey the next step through local community contacts, sometimes people need to travel far and wide to find where they're going. Here are a few places you can contact as further resources:

1) Contemplative Outreach National Office — an outgrowth of the "Centering Prayer" movement, and particularly Father Thomas Keating's work. Primarily Catholic in its roots, but open to others. P.O. Box 737, Butler, NJ 07405. Phone: 201-838-3384.

2) Pendle Hill — a Quaker retreat center with a strong interfaith history. 338 Plush Mill Road, Wallingford, PA 19086-6099. Phone: 800-742-3150.

3) Shalem Institute — an ecumenical Christian center headed by an Episcopal priest, Tilden Edwards. Other full-time staff members include the well-known psychiatrist and spiritual writer Gerald May. 5430 Grosnevor Lane, Bethesda, MD 20814. Phone: 301-897-7334. www.shalom.org.

4) Retreats International — a Catholic clearinghouse of retreat information that offers programs and publications, including a directory listing about 600 retreat centers. P.O. Box 1067, Notre Dame, IN 46556. Phone: 800-556-4532. e-mail: retreats.retreats.1@nd.edu   website: www.Retreatsintl.org

For a useful listing of many other centers for prayer and meditation, you may wish to consult *Sanctuaries: A Guide to Lodgings in Monasteries, Abbeys, and Retreats*, written by Jack and Marcia Kelly. Most of the places described are "contemplative communities which invite people to share their life and prayer", and generally they welcome people of all faiths, though they themselves grow out of particular traditions. Christian, Buddhist, Hindu, Sufi, and Jewish communities are represented. There are three books in this superb series, all published by Bell Tower in New York: *The Complete United States*, *The Northeast*, and *The West Coast and Southwest*.

Bell Tower of Harmony Books is an imprint of Crown Publishers which in turn is a division of Random House: Phonne: 800-638-6460. www.randomhouse.com

Further Reading

The following list includes only books currently in print at the time of this writing — for the purpose of providing suggestions that will be most easily accessible to the reader, and also to keep the list within bounds. All prices included are U.S. list prices as of September 1998.

Books of Mother Teresa's Spiritual Wisdom:
These works can be divided into two categories: relatively small "gems" (volumes aimed at offering a good but limited sampling of thoughts) and books striving to be more definitive. All are explicitly Christ-centered (some more centrally than others), and all treat Mother Teresa's thoughts on prayer as one of at least a few themes. Primarily biographical works are beyond the scope of this bibliography.

Books preceded by a single asterix are widely available at many bookstores. Those with two asterixes are available mainly on the shelves of Christian, and especially Catholic, bookstores. Of course, most can be ordered through your local bookstore, and all can be ordered directly from the publishers.

Slimmer Books:

In the Heart of the World: Thoughts, Prayers, and Stories (New World Library, Novato CA, 1997. Hardcover, 144 pages, $16. Phone: 800-972-6657). A fine gift edition of luminous selections edited by Becky Benenate. The press also offers a Mother Teresa web site: www.mother-teresa.com

Meditations from A Simple Path (Ballantine Books, New York, 1996. Hardcover, 88 pages, $10. Ballantine, a division of Random House. Phone: 800-638-6460. www.randomhouse.-com). Excerpts from the larger book, *A Simple Path* (see below), but this one is composed entirely of Mother Teresa's own words and spiritual teaching. Another lovingly produced gift edition brimming with Mother Teresa's timeless pearls of wisdom.

In My Own Words (Gramercy Books, NY, 1996. Hardcover, 109 pages, $5.95. Gramercy, a division of Random House. Phone: 800-638-6460. www.randomhouse.com). Pearls arranged according to fifteen themes. Edited by Jose Luis Gonzalez-Balado, one of the long-standing editors of Mother's written works, and especially for a hardcover, a real bargain.

**Words to Love By,* compiled by Frank J. Cunningham (Ave Maria Press, Notre Dame IN, 1983, Paperback, 80 pages, $5.95. Phone: 800-282-1865). Poetically presented text highlighting the glories and challenges of Mother Teresa's message, with frequent photos. Reasonably priced.

**The Best Gift Is Love: Meditations by Mother Teresa* (Servant Publications, Ann Arbor MI, 1982. Paperback, 120 pages, $8.99. Phone: 800-458-8505). Like *Words to Love By* in its basic approach — highlights of Mother Teresa's instructions and reflections, poetically presented on the page, with many photos interspersed. Compiled by Sean-Patrick Lovett.

**Blessings of Love.* (Servant Publications, Ann Arbor MI, 1996. Paperback, 128 pages, $5.99. Phone: 800-458-8505).A sweet collection of brief inspirational sayings gathered from several of the other Servant Publication works listed below. Edited by Nancy Sabbag.

149

A Gift for God: Prayers and Meditations (Harper San Francisco, San Francisco, U.S. edition 1975. Paperback, 78 pages, $11. Phone: 800-331-3761. www.harpercollins.com). One of the earliest short collections of reflections, and a kind of companion work to Malcolm Muggeridge's classic 1971 biographical sketch *Something Beautiful for God*, also still in print.

Larger Works:

No Greater Love (New World Library, Novato CA, 1997. Hardcover, 206 pages, $21. For publisher information, see *In the Heart of the World* listing above). A wonderfully comprehensive and accessible collection organized in eleven themes followed first by a conversation with Mother Teresa, then by a biographical sketch. Edited by Becky Benenate and Joseph Durepos, Foreword by Thomas Moore. Also now available in the U.S. in a Spanish edition (*El amor mas grande*).

A Simple Path (Ballantine Books, New York, 1995. Hardcover, 202 pages, $20. For publisher information, see *Meditations from a Simple Path* above). A perfect introduction to Mother Teresa's work and teachings, this book contains not only Mother Teresa's spiritual principles but also the experiences of them by other members of her Order and volunteers. Compiled and introduced by Lucinda Vardey. Contains an Appendix with important dates in Mother Teresa's life and another with information on the Order she founded, the Missionaries of Charity.

The Joy in Loving: A Guide to Daily Living with Mother Teresa (Viking Penguin, New York, original copyright in India 1996. Hardcover, 438 pages, $19.95. Phone: 212-366-2000 www.penguin.com). Reflections, one for each day of the year, covering a wide range of topics. Two long-time associates of

Mother Teresa's, Jaya Chaliha and Father Edward Le Joly, compiled this stirring collection. Father Le Joly, who was Mother Teresa's spiritual advisor and the author of a major biography of Mother Teresa, also provides a detailed introduction to the history of her work. The thoughts are presented as short sayings in stanza form. While not organized by theme, contains a useful thematic index.

**Love: A Fruit Always in Season* (Ignatius Press, San Francisco, 1987. Paperback, 260 pages, $9.95. Phone: 800-651-1531). A far-ranging book of daily meditations, arranged according to the Catholic calendar and also by theme. An excellent selection edited by Dorothy S. Hunt, drawing upon many earlier works, all of which are cited — a real help for knowing where the meditations first appeared.

Total Surrender (Servant Publications, Ann Arbor, 1985. Paperback, 157 pages, $6.99. For publisher information on this and the next four books, see *The Best Gift is Love* listing above). A rich spiritual sourcebook of excerpts from the constitution of Mother Teresa's Order as well as her instructions and letters within the Order. Comprehensive. Edited by Brother Angelo Devananda.

**Jesus: The Word to be Spoken: Meditations for Every Day of the Year* (Servant Publications, Ann Arbor MI, 1986. Paperback, 158 pages, $6.99). Another well-done collection by Brother Angelo Devananda, this one arranged in calendar form.

**One Heart Full of Love* (Servant Publications, Ann Arbor, original copyright in Spain 1984. Paperback, 150 pages, $5.99). A variety of rousing talks, interviews, and correspondence, with an emphasis on loving the poor and the blessings of sharing. Edited by Jose Luis Gonzalez-Balado.

Loving Jesus (Servant Publications, Ann Arbor, 1991. Paperback, 168 pages, $6.99). Another collection of dynamic addresses edited by Jose Luis Gonzalez-Balado, including a long interview and a biographical sketch.

Heart of Joy: The Transforming Power of Self-Giving (Servant Publications, Ann Arbor MI, 1987. Paperback, 149 pages, $6.99). Yet another worthwhile Gonzalez-Balado compendium of Mother Teresa's words, gathered from a variety of sources.

Prayertimes with Mother Teresa: A New Adventure in Prayer Involving Scripture, Mother Teresa, and You (Image Books, New York, 1989. Paperback, 166 pages, $8.95. Image Books, an imprint of Doubleday. Phone: 800-223-6834). For each week of the year, a passage from the Bible, a story by or about Mother Teresa, and a spiritual reflection from her. Edited by Eileen Egan and Kathleen Egan. The main text is followed by a "seven-day retreat" section with suggested prayers, litanies and meditations.

Works of Love Are Works of Peace: Mother Teresa of Calcutta and the Missionaries of Charity (Ignatius Press, San Francisco, 1996) Hardcover, 224 pages, $34.95. Phone: 800-651-1531). One of the stunning books of photos available, this one has selections of Mother Teresa's counsel, including a letter on prayer, as well as a full collection of the Order's prayers.

Among other closely related books of interest, perhaps most notable is *Suffering into Joy* by Eileen and Kathleen Egan, (Servant Publications), which contains passages from Mother Teresa's teachings. See above for publisher's information.

Further Books on Prayer:

There are many good books on prayer. The list below is far from exhaustive but includes some of this editor's favorite ones. They are restricted to books entirely about prayer, rather than ones that may contain a chapter or two on the subject. The emphasis is on practical, down-to-earth guides that are most likely to further the actual practice of prayer. Books of prayers are not included.

Books addressed equally to Christians and non-Christians: There are fairly few of these around!

Larry Dossey, *Prayer Is Good Medicine* (Harper San Francisco, San Francisco CA, 1996. Paperback, 249 pages, $12). The author, who wrote the Foreword to *Everything Starts from Prayer* and is a highly regarded physician and thinker, describes this book as "a heart-to-heart talk." Dossey wisely discusses prayer and common misconceptions about prayer, with a special focus on the relations between prayer, healing and science. The longest of four sections is called "How to Pray." (See also Dossey's more detailed, scholarly *Healing Words: The Power of Prayer and the Practice of Medicine* and his more recent thoughtful book *Be Careful What You Pray For*.

On this interface between prayer and medicine, probably the other three best-known writers are Bernie Siegel, M.D., Herbert Benson, M.D., and Joan Borysenko, Ph.D. All worth reading.

James P. Carse, *The Silence of God: Meditations on Prayer* (HarperSan Francisco, San Francisco, 1985. Paperback, 107 pages, $11. (See publisher information under Dossey's book above). An NYU professor of religion brings simplicity together with philosophic depth to his writings on prayer. Four graceful, grounded meditations about speaking to God from the heart. Incisive and heart-centered.

Richard Chilson, *You Shall Not Want: A Spiritual Journey Based on the Psalms* (Ave Maria Press, Notre Dame IN, 1996. Paperback, 212 pages, $6.95. Phone: 800-282-1865). A guide to prayer using brief selections and phrases from the psalms arranged for the thirty days in a month. Gently presented. From Ave Maria's "30 Days with a Great Spiritual Teacher" Series, whose other volumes are also recommended.

Matthew Fox, *On Becoming a Musical Mystical Bear: Spirituality American Style* (Paulist Press, New York, 1972. Paperback, 156 pages, $9.95. Phone: 800-836-3161. Website: www.ulistpress.com). Simultaneously whimsical and serious, Fox takes a contemplative activist's look at "what prayer is" and "what prayer isn't." He presents his ideas of "creation spirituality" in the process, and whereas he doesn't present prayer here in the precise "how to" terms of a spiritual practice, he underscores points that many people inclined to withdraw from the world in the name of "dedicated spiritual practice" all too easily overlook.

Dale Salwak (editor) *The Power of Prayer* is due out by New World Library in October 1998. A multifaith anthology that includes contributions by Mother Teresa and by this editor. Also look for *The Flowering of the Soul: Prayers Written by Women* (Lucinda Vardey, editor) due out in the spring of 1999 by Ballantine, which offers an approach to praying through the experiences and counsel of women from diverse traditions, including Mother Teresa.

Christian books on prayer:

If you don't feel entirely comfortable calling yourself "Christian", yet you begin to read inspirational Christian writings, I have a suggestion. You might want to consider a different name that works for you, if the term "Christian" doesn't feel like a full fit, when you come across "Christian" on the page. Substitutes might include "a truly good person," "an open and growing person" "a holy person," "a person trying her or his very best," "a student of prayer," or "a sincere spiritual seeker." Where devotion to Jesus is discussed, this may not quite hit the mark, but where universal insights about devotion and prayer and inner work are the subjects, it will. There may be some legitimate objections to this idea. Nonetheless, it seems that often "Christian" or other designations like "Jew" or "Muslim" are used within their own groups as synonyms for "a truly good person" or the like and when used as such are a residue of a more provincial era. I believe it's important to try at times to open ourselves to writings of our brothers and sisters in other cultures, and to translate basic insights across these differing traditions, both for our own sake and for the sake of those on these other paths. This is especially crucial, perhaps, in our day and age.

Metropolitan Anthony (Anthony Bloom), Volume in *The Modern Spirituality Series* (Templegate, Springfield IL, 1987. Paperback, 94 pages, $4.95. Phone: 800-367-4844. www.Templegate.com). The most concise introduction to a first-rate, living writer on prayer. The author is a former medical doctor and French resistance fighter turned Russian Orthodox priest and church leader. ("Metropolitan" is something like "Cardinal" in the Eastern Orthodox church.) The book is an offering of page-long selections from earlier works, and it contains a convenient reference to all of these works at the end, among which *Beginning to Pray* and *Living Prayer* are especially recommended. Also reasonably priced.

Douglas V. Steere, *Dimensions of Prayer* (Upper Room Books, Nashville TN, original copyright 1962. Hardcover, 106 pages, $13.95. Upper Room Books Phone: 800-972-0433; www. upperroom.org). A succinct and down-to-earth classic on prayer by a scholar and Quaker leader. Steere, a professor of philosophy at Haverford, was the main Quaker representative at Vatican II and an early pioneer of ecumenical dialogue with Buddhists and Hindus. A document he wrote for Quaker organizational purposes eventually became the blueprint for the Peace Corps. He shares with Metropolitan Anthony a great gift for the telling vignette.

Thomas Keating, *Open Mind, Open Heart: The Contemplative Dimension of the Gospel* (Element Books, Rockport, Maine. Paperback, $12.95. Phone: 800-331-4624). In 1975, a few Catholic monks developed a method called "Centering Prayer" and devised ways of teaching it. Father Keating provides one of the clearest step-by-step descriptions of this approach, which simplifies lofty, age-old spiritual wisdom meaningfully for our time. Among its best points, Keating offers sound and straightforward advice regarding "distracting thoughts" and inner obstacles to praying in general. It should be emphasized that the approach outlined is a high form of practice that isn't meant to exclude other forms. See also M. Basil Pennington's *Centering Prayer* (Image Books, New York. Paperback, $8.95) and William A. Meninger's *The*

Loving Search for God, (Continuum, New York, 1994. Paperback, $11.95. Phone: 800-937-5557).

Ken Gire (editor), *Between Heaven and Earth: Prayers and Reflections That Celebrate An Intimate God* (Harper San Francisco, San Francisco, 1997. Hardcover, 384 pages, $22.) An unusually good collection of meaningful reflections about prayer interspersed with some prayers themselves. Passages are mainly from well-known writers like C.S. Lewis, Richard Foster, Abraham Joshua Heschel, Larry Dossey, Dietrich Bonhoeffer, and many others you may well recognize. Various faith traditions are included, though the sources are primarily Christian. (See publisher information under Dossey's book above.)

Among the numerous other noteworthy Christian books about prayer as spiritual practice in print, please bear in mind the following titles: Brother David Steindl-Rast, *Gratefulness, The Heart of Prayer: An Approach to Life in Fullness*; Richard J. Foster, *Prayer: Finding the Heart's True Home*; Tilden Edwards, *Living in the Presence: Spiritual Exercises to Open Your Life to the Awareness of God*; Martin Helldorfer, *Prayer When It's Hard to Pray*; Thomas Kelly, *A Testament of Devotion*; Richard J. Foster and James Bryan Smith, *Devotional Classics*; Thomas Merton, *Contemplative Prayer* (the introduction by Zen master Thich Nhat Hanh and foreword by Douglas Steere are treats in themselves); Gabriel Galache, *Praying Body and Soul: Methods and Practices of Anthony De Mello*; John R. Yungblut, *Rediscovering Prayer*; and Patricia Loring, *Listening Spirituality* (available from Pendle Hill: 800-742-3150). Most of these books can lead the reader in turn to other enriching works.

Pendle Hill (listed above) is one good catalog source of books on prayer. Other useful catalogs can be ordered from Templegate (800-367-4844), St. Mary's Press (800-282-1865), Servant Books (800-315-8505), Upper Room Books (800-972-0433), Paulist Press (800-836-3161), Ave Maria Press (800-282-1865), and Liguori Publications (800-464-2555).

Jewish books on prayer:
The note about the word "Christian" above applies equally to the word "Jew." Even as we honor our own traditions, we need to remember that historically a wounded antagonism has separated groups of believers and has colored their views of other groups. We need to remember, and we need to do our utmost, to acknowledge it in ourselves, work with it, and slowly (or immediately!) get beyond it. Let's not, in any case, deprive ourselves of the inspiration and insight contained in other sacred traditions, even in works purportedly aimed only at a single group.

Arthur Green and Barry W. Holtz (editors and translators), *Your Word Is Fire: The Hasidic Masters on Contemplative Prayer* (Jewish Lights Publishing, Woodstock VT, 1977. Paperback, 152 pages, $14.95. Phone: 800-962-4544. www.Jewishlights. com). Parables and sayings from the extraordinary Hasidic literature on prayer, presented in verse form, with a brief introduction that serves admirably as a summary of Hasidic thought. Edited by two leaders of the Jewish renewal movement.

Yitzhak Buxbaum, *Real Davvening: Jewish Prayer as a Form of Meditation for Beginning and Experienced Davveners* (Jewish Spirit, New York, 1996. Paperback, 42 pages. $7.95. Phone: 718-539-5978). "Davvening" is a Jewish word for praying. This booklet explicitly aims to provide the reader simple hints for meeting God in prayer. In other words, it offers an explanation of the spiritual side of Jewish worship and contains simple traditional techniques for how to experience God's presence during communal devotional services. Readily applicable to other traditions. See also the author's much more detailed work, *Jewish Spiritual Practices*, especially chapters five and six.

Rabbi Nachman, *Tsohar* ("Light") (Breslov Research Institute, New York, 1986. Paperback, 64 pages, $3.00. Breslov Research Institute: 800-33-273768 or 914-425-4258). The 18th and 19th century Hasidic tradition is a wonderful source of practical wisdom about prayer, and Rabbi Nachman of Breslov (or "Bratslav") was one of its greatest teachers. This booklet, which centers on the power of "just one true word" in prayer, is one of several valuable booklets published by The Breslov Research Institute. Other recommended ones include *Outpouring of the Soul* and *Restore My Soul*.

Sidney Greenberg, *A Treasury of Thoughts on Jewish Prayer* (Jason Aronson, Northvale NJ, 1989. Paperback, 238 pages, $25. Phone: 800-782-0015. www.aronson.com). A rich anthology of short selections from many sources, including the Talmud, the Hasidic masters, and contemporary thinkers. These are intelligently selected and heartfelt passages with a scope wider than the question "how to pray" — but consistently good food for thought and inspiration for worship.

159

Islamic Books on Prayer

Prayer is central to Islamic spirituality. One of the five "pillars" of Islam is daily prayer (*salat*), which consists of a series of movements enacted while reciting suras, or chapters, from the Qur'an. Other forms of prayer include *du'a*, or personal entreaties and petitions; *dhikr*, or meditative remembrance on a sacred word or phrase; and *munajat*, or devotional conversations between the lover and the divine beloved. A helpful introduction and sourcebook to prayer in Islam is:

Constance Padwick, *Muslim Devotions: A Study of Prayer Manuals in Common Use* (Element Books, Paperback, $19.99, See publisher's information under Keating's book above).

To readers of other religions: My research has led to fewer works devoted to prayer from Eastern and native traditions. For example, although prayer is naturally emphasized in Buddhist and Hindu traditions, there is a strong emphasis on meditative practices. Thus prayer often takes the form of repeating sacred phrases from holy books (popularly known in the West as mantras). I would like to include books on prayer from non-Western faith traditions in future editions of this book and encourage readers send me any suggestions in care of White Cloud Press, P.O. Box 3400, Ashland, Oregon 97520.

Best wishes in your search. I can attest to the fact that there are unforeseen treasures awaiting you.

Sources & Acknowledgments

Wholehearted appreciation is due Sister Priscilla and the Missionaries of Charity in Calcutta for granting permission for the compilation of this collection and for their input in the process. A portion of the receipts from the sale of this book will go to the Missionaries of Charity. For more information on the work of the Order, contact its U.S. houses: 335 E. 145th St., Bronx NY 10451 and 312 29th St., San Francisco CA 94131.

I have tried to leave no stone unturned in my efforts to obtain permissions. If there are oversights I would request that the aggrieved party contact me so that I may get it right for possible future editions.

It should be mentioned that there is considerable overlap in Mother Teresa's writings. I have cited one source for each passage in this volume, but many of these meditations can be found in a few different books.

Where sources have been printed in hardcover and paperback editions, the page numbers below refer to the hardcover edition.

Grateful acknowledgments to

New World Library for permission to reprint from the following seven works: *No Greater Love* (called simply "Love" below) (New World Library, NY, 1997), edited by Becky Benenate and Joseph Durepos; *Total Surrender* (called simply "Surrender" below) (Servant Books, Ann Arbor, 1985), edited by Brother Angela Devananda; *Jesus, the Word to Be Spoken: Prayers and Meditations for Every Day of the Year* (called simply "Jesus" below) (Servant Books, Ann Arbor, 1986), compiled by Brother Angelo Devananda; *Heart of Joy* (called simply "Heart" below) (Servant Books, Ann Arbor, 1987), edited by Jose Luis Gonzalez-Balado; *One Heart Full of Love* (called simply "Full" below) (Servant Books, Ann Arbor, 1984), edited by Jose Luis Gonzalez-Balado; *Loving Jesus* (called simply "Loving" below) (Servant Books, Ann Arbor, 1991), edited by Jose Luis Gonzalez-Balado; *Suffering into Joy* (called simply "Suffering" below) (Servant Books, Ann Arbor, 1996), written by Eileen Egan and Kathleen Egan;

to Penguin India for permission to reprint from *The Joy in Loving* (called simply "Joy" below) (Viking Penguin, NY, original copyright 1996), compiled by Jaya Chaliha and Edward Le Joly;

to Ballantine Books for permission to reprint from *A Simple Path* (called simply "Path" below) (Ballantine, NY, 1995), compiled by Lucinda Vardey;

to SPCK (the Society to Promote Christian Knowledge) for permission to reprint from the following two works: *Life in the Spirit* (simply called "Spirit" below) (Harper and Row, San Francisco, 1983), edited by Kathryn Spink; *I Need Souls like You* (called simply "Souls" below) (Harper and Row, San Francisco, 1984), edited by Kathryn Spink;

to HarperCollins and HarperCollins United Kingdom for permission to reprint from the following five works: *My Life for the Poor* (called simply "Life" below) (Harper and Row, New York, 1985), edited by Jose Luis Gonzalez-Balado and Janet N. Playfoot; *The Love of Christ: Spiritual Counsels, Mother Teresa of Calcutta* (called simply "Christ" below) (Harper and Row, San Francisco, 1982), edited by Georges Gorree and Jean Barbier; *A Gift for God: Mother Teresa of*

162

Calcutta (called simply "Gift" below) (Harper and Row, New York, 1975); *Mother Teresa: Her People and Her Work* (called simply "People" below) (Harper and Row, NY, 1976), edited by Desmond Doig; *Mother Teresa of Calcutta: A Biography* (called simply "Calcutta" below) (Harper and Row, San Francisco, 1983), by Edward Le Joly;

to Liguori Publications and Jose Luis Gonzalez-Balado for permission to reprint from the following two works: *In My Own Words* (called simply "Words" below) (Liguori, Liguori Missouri, 1996), compiled by Jose Luis Gonzalez-Balado (page numbers in the new Gramercy Books edition are noted with "GB" preceding); *Always the Poor* (called simply "Always" below) (Liguori, Liguori, Missouri, 1980), edited by Jose Luis Gonzalez-Balado;

to Ave Maria Press for permission to reprint from *Words to Love By* (called simply "Words" below) (Ave Maria Press, Notre Dame, Indiana, 1983), compiled by Frank J. Cunningham.

Other Sources

Love: A Fruit Always in Season, edited by Dorothy Hunt, (called simply "Fruit" below) (Ignatius Press, San Francisco, 1987).

Works of Love Are Works of Peace: Mother Teresa of Calcutta and the Missionaries of Charity, edited with photographs by Michael Collopy (called simply "Works" below) (Ignatius Press, San Francisco, 1996).

Mother Teresa by Navin Chawla, (called simply "Mother" below) (Element Books, Rockport, Maine, 1992).

Such a Vision of the Street by Eileen Egan, (called simply "Vision" below) (Doubleday, NY, 1985).

Sources of Specific Passages:

p. 1 : *Joy*, p. 43

p. 2, top passage: *Jesus*, p. 21

p. 2, bottom passage: *Spirit*, p. 82

p. 3: *Surrender*, p. 109

p. 4, top passage: *Heart*, p. 98

p. 4, bottom passage: *Jesus*, p. 74

p. 5, top passage: *Joy*, p. 325

p. 5, bottom passage: *Path*, p. 19

p. 6: *Spirit*, pp. 38-39

p. 7, top passage: *Christ*, p. 48

p. 7, bottom passage: *Spirit*, p. 65

p. 8: *Calcutta*, pp. 227-28

p. 9, top passage: *Spirit*, p. 72

p. 9, bottom passage: *Heart*, p. 123

p. 10: *Joy*, p. 96

p. 11: *Spirit*, p. 82

p. 12, top passage: *Joy*, p. 159

p. 12, bottom passage: *Joy*, p. 260

p. 13: *In*, p. 103 (GB: p. 51)

p. 14, top passage: *In*, p. 104 (GB: p. 51)

p. 14, bottom passage: *Surrender*, p. 98

p. 15: *In*, p. 36 (GB: p. 11)

p. 19, top passage: *Christ*, p. 8

p. 19, bottom passage: *Life*, p. 100

p. 20: *Christ*, p. 8

p. 21, top passage: *Life*, p. 101

p. 21, bottom passage: *Joy*, p. 114

p. 22, top passage: *Joy*, p. 127

p. 22, bottom passage: *Surrender*, p. 106

p. 23, top and bottom passages: *Love*, pp. 9-10

p. 24: *Love*, p. 8

p. 25: *Surrender*, p. 106

p. 26: *Surrender*, p. 108

p. 27: *Love*, p. 10-11

p. 28: *Joy*, p. 149

p. 29: *Life*, p. 101

p. 30, top passage: *Spirit*, p. 20

p. 30, bottom passage: *Jesus*, p. 3

p. 31: *Surrender*, p. 110

p. 35, top passage: *Full*, p. 123

p. 35, bottom passage, 1st 4 sentences: *Life*, p. 104

p. 35, bottom passage, last 2 sentences: *Words*, p. 40

p. 36: *Path*, p. 13

p. 37: *Suffering*, pp. 34-35

p. 38: *Surrender*, p. 100 and p. 101

p. 39: *Joy*, p. 108 (". . . that you may preach without preaching" derives from a prayer written by a 19th century English theologian and cardinal, John Henry Newman. In its entirety it's about half a page, but it reads in part, "Let me preach you without preaching, not by my words but by my example . . . ." Mother Teresa loved this prayer, and the Missionaries of Charity pray it every day.)

p. 40, top passage: *Path*, p. 8

p. 40, bottom passage: *Spirit*, p. 17

p. 41, top passage: *Life*, p. 104

p. 41, bottom passage: *People*, p. 166

p. 42, top passage: *Christ*, p. 20

p. 42, bottom passage: *Word*, p. 8

p. 43, top passage: *Path*, p. 20

p. 43, bottom passage: *Path*, p. 15

p. 44, top and bottom passages: *Spirit*, p. 30

p. 45: *Love*, pp. 4-5

p. 46: *Heart*, p. 1-2

p. 47: *Jesus*, p. 6

p. 48, top passage: *Path*, p. 8

p. 48, bottom passage, top 1/2: *Vision*, p. 328

p. 48, bottom passage, bottom 1/2: *Calcutta*, p. 18

p. 49: *Life*, p. 98

p. 50: *In*, p. 28 (GB: p. 7)

p. 51: *Gift*, pp. 37-38

p. 52: *Love*, p. 113

p. 53, top passage: *Spirit*, p. 48

p. 82, bottom passage: *People*, p. 145-46

p. 83: *Path*, p. 14

p. 84: *Path*, p. 14

p. 85, top passage: *Path*, p. 14

p. 85, bottom passage: *Path*, p. 14

p. 86: *Path*, p. 20

p. 87: *Path*, pp. 14-15

p. 88, top passage: *Joy*, p. 107

p. 88, bottom passage: *Fruit*, p. 110

p. 89, top passage: *Spirit*, p. 35

p. 89, bottom passage: *Spirit*, p. 35

p. 90, top passage: *Joy*, p. 136

p. 90, bottom passage: *Christ*, p. 103

p. 91, top passage: *Spirit*, p. 68

p. 91, bottom passage: *Jesus*, p. 121

p. 92 (all but the first line, which recurs throughout Mother Teresa's writings): *Joy*, p. 103 (in this passage, Mother Teresa has drawn from Isaiah 43:1-4 and 49:15-16)

p. 93, top passage: *Joy*, p. 127

p. 93, bottom passage: *Love*, p. 4

p. 94: *Love*, p. 6. (Compare St. Augustine's beautiful words: "My whole heart I lay upon the altar of thy praise, a holocaust of praise I offer to Thee. Let the flame of Thy love set on fire my whole heart; may I wholly burn toward Thee, wholly on fire toward Thee, wholly Thee as though set aflame by Thee." Quoted in Douglas V. Steere, *Beginning from Within*, p. 110.)

p. 99, top passage: *Surrender*, p. 103

p. 99, bottom passage: *Joy*, p. 273

p. 100, top passage: *Life*, p. 100

p. 100, bottom passage: *Love*, p. 7

p. 101: *Surrender*, p. 106

p. 102: *Surrender*, p. 111

p. 103, top passage: *Christ*, p. 9

p. 103, bottom passage: *Surrender*, p. 108. (The last sentence is from Psalm 46:10.)

p. 107, top passage: *Surrender*, p. 107

p. 107, middle passage: *Life*, p. 101. (A lovely way of putting what the psalmist, Meister Eckhart, St. Augustine, St. Thomas Aquinas, and many others have said. Any claim of originality would have been antithetical to Mother Teresa.)

p. 107, bottom passage: *Spirit*, p. 45

p. 108, top passage: *Words*, p. 160

p. 108, middle passage: *Christ*, p. 52

p. 108, bottom passage: *Spirit*, p. 45

p. 109, top passage: *Words*, p. 44

p. 109, bottom passage: *Heart*, p. 82

p. 110, top passage: *Path*, p. 7

p. 110, bottom passage: *Surrender*, pp. 111-112

p. 111, top passage: *Jesus*, p. 59

p. 111, bottom passage: *Joy*, p. 238

p. 112: *Jesus*, p. 57

p. 113: *Surrender*, p. 110

p. 114: *Words*, p. 40

p. 115, top passage: *Joy*, p. 329

p. 115, bottom passage: *Path*, p. 8

p. 116, top passage: *Love*, pp. 7-8

p. 116, bottom passage: *Jesus*, p. 4

p. 117: *Always*, p. 7

p. 118, top passage: *Heart*, p. 90

p. 118, bottom passage: *Christ*, pp. 46 and 44

p. 119: *Love*, p. 9

p. 120: *Jesus*, p. 68

p. 121, top passage: *Jesus*, p. 88

p. 121, bottom passage: *Mother*, p. xxiv

p. 122: *Joy*, p. 114

p. 123: *Joy*, p. 142

p. 124: *Joy*, p. 137

p. 125, top passage: *Life*, p. 49

p. 125, bottom passage: *Joy*, p. 145

p. 126: *Spirit*, p. 69

p. 127: *Words*, p. 90 (GB: p. 42)

p. 128: *Joy*, p. 128

Further Acknowledgments

First, I'd like to say that there are so many people who have helped out one way or another with this collection that it would require a small book in itself to thank each of them with minimal adequacy. Instead, let me simply offer sincere thanks now for all these nameless helpers. You know who you are.

There are a number of people who played critical roles. Heartfelt gratitude to my publisher Steven Scholl and to the three literary agents involved at various stages — Kim Witherspoon, Gideon Weil, and Michele Rubin.

169

Many thanks are due all of my family, and especially my wife Laura and our three children Charles and Joe and Marguerite, for bearing with the time this work has required of me. I know they often felt, with considerable accuracy, that they were suddenly sharing our family life with an unusual stranger from a foreign land.

A particular group in the publishing world did work absolutely crucial to my own — the editors and publishers of earlier compilations of Mother Teresa's wisdom, including Dorothy Hunt, Lucinda Vardey, Becky Benenate, Father Edward Le Joly, Bert Ghezzi, Jose Luis Gonzalez-Balado, Kathryn Spink, Brother Angelo Devananda, Eileen Egan, Kathleen Egan, Joseph Durepos, Desmond Doig, and Jaya Chaliha. The first five in this group gave generously of their time to me directly, providing further assistance to make this book possible. Others in the publishing world whose enthusiasm for the project was a real impetus included Peter Edelman, Kris Kleimann, Amy Edelman, Paul Cash, and Marcia Broucek. Marcia also reminded me of the important gender issues involved with Mother Teresa's language.

Grateful thanks to Janet Murphy and all her staff at the Hastings-on-Hudson Public Library, for their endless interlibrary loan efforts. Rowie Edelman and Debbie Boylan at Good Yarns Bookstore also gave valuable assistance.

Thanks also to Sarah Sprague, Aaron Silverman, and Molly Maguire for their support of this book.

Finally, I'd like to express my deep gratitude to the three people who, in my own pre-teen and teen years, introduced me to the world of prayer: Annie Lee, Frank J. Bertino, and Rudi.